A Fresh Understanding of
ISRAEL

Seven Questions and Seven Responses

Edited by
ADAM RAFFELL & JACOB VINCE

malcolm down
PUBLISHING

21 20 19 18 17 16   7 6 5 4 3 2 1

First published 2017 by Malcolm Down Publishing Ltd.
www.malcolmdown.co.uk

British Library Cataloguing in Publication Data
A catalogue record for this book is available from the British Library.

ISBN 978-1-910786-62-8

Thanks to Roy Thurley, Sian Treharne
and Chris Moxon for their assistance in proofreading.

Cover design by Esther Kotecha
Cover image used under license from Shutterstock

Printed and Bound in Great Britain by Bell & Bain Ltd, Glasgow

CONTENTS

Introduction

A Fresh Understanding of Israel was commissioned by an alliance of Christian ministries and organisations, called Love Never Fails, who share a common calling to serve both Israel ('Israel' encompassing the Jewish people and the State of Israel in the broadest sense) and the in-grafted church. What it seeks to sketch, through a series of responses to seven questions, is a picture of Israel which emerges through the eyes of Christian readers of the Bible in the twenty-first century.

All of our contributors have in various ways been involved in the Jewish-Christian relationship from the Christian side and therefore this book represents an attempt to share with others the interpretations of Scripture which have underpinned our various ministries. These are dubbed *'Fresh'* because they are constructing a positive alternative to some of the supercessionist assumptions which can all too often, and even inadvertently, infiltrate our thinking, theology and exegesis from time to time. The prevailing Christian interpretation of the Pauline corpus in particular has emphasised a negative assessment of Jewish 'Law', and the thinking of this book falls in line with the important revisions that have been challenging such interpretations over the past few decades.

Our purpose was to build upon the foundation of what

supremely unites us: the Old and New Testament scriptures themselves and our shared faith in Jesus Christ, the Messiah of Israel. We resolved therefore to write our responses referring only to scriptural texts. Each chapter was composed independently by the contributor in question, with a few explanatory footnotes having been added by the editors in some cases. A broad reading list of literature which has been formative in shaping many of our interpretations is also included at the end.

We are advocating for a broader recognition, within the church and amongst Christians, of God's ongoing relationship with Israel – the Jewish people – which we pray will enable dialogue, understanding and relationship to flourish between Jews and Christians. This is the only appropriate context within which Jews and Christians can do things which neither of us can do properly alone: things like coming to terms with the wrongdoings of the past, resisting antisemitism in the present, building the kingdom of God, recognising the meaning and significance of the modern State of Israel, and exploring the New Testament's claims about Jesus.

Although we share a basic assumption that the State of Israel represents a provision for the Jewish people which is in accordance with the promises of Scripture, it is possibly discernible that we are not entirely theologically, exegetically or politically homogenous. The reader is encouraged to weigh and to digest our responses as part of their own encounter with the God of Israel and Jesus Christ his Son, our Lord, as revealed to us in the Bible.

1. What Made the People of Israel Significant in the First Place?

BY STEPHEN BRIGGS

> From beginning to end, the Bible reveals that one of God's greatest desires is that human beings, insignificant as we are, might enter into such a relationship with him that he might call us 'his people'.
>
> David Watson (Church Leader)

Israel. Everyone the world over has an opinion about the Mediterranean State created by the international community in 1948. Why in the twenty-first century does such a small nation have such a global impact? What is it that matters so much to otherwise disinterested politicians and journalists?

The political question is about both the land and the people. So when we talk about Israel, we must at least, to some extent, include the history of the Jewish people. Vast empires have come and gone, ruled over the 'promised land' and then vanished from sight. Indo-European languages have disappeared. Yet somehow this tiny group, which has been spread literally to the four corners of the earth, has survived with even its language still intact. It is remarkable.

The significance of Israel throughout history is also

astounding. The Jewish people play a role in so many cultures, time periods and geographic locations – identified as the people who carry the name 'Israel' as part of their inheritance. Their journey is a narrative so remarkable that it has changed the course of world history.

It is a journey that began thousands of years ago. Almighty God, after the fall of man in the Garden of Eden, set about the process of restoring mankind to himself. This was the beginning of the answer to the question of defining Israel's significance in the eternal purpose of God and in our world today.

God's character never changes. He states, 'I the LORD do not change. So you, the descendants of Jacob, are not destroyed (Mal. 3:6). And, 'Jesus Christ is the same yesterday and today and forever' (Heb. 13:8).

The God we serve is identified in the New Testament (or 'New Covenant')[1] and the Old Testament (or 'Old Covenant') as the same one God, a God whose character never changes. It is his process of restoring mankind and his unchanging promises that precisely shape the reasons why Israel's status in world history has been so significant.

It began with a statement which God made to Abram[2] saying, 'I will bless those who bless you, and whoever curses you I will curse; and all peoples on earth will be blessed through you' (Gen. 12:3).

This was not merely a throwaway comment but rather a watershed statement in history. These few words began the exciting journey of redemption, for *all* mankind, for all time. It is on this promise that the 'New Covenant' is built: namely that through Abraham's seed the Messiah would come.

In Genesis it says that the Lord made a covenant with Abram, saying, 'The whole land of Canaan, where you now reside as a foreigner, I will give as an everlasting possession to you and your descendants after you; and I will be their God' (Gen. 17:8).

This covenant is repeated in Genesis 22:16-18, 26:2-5 and 28:13-15. Psalm 105:5-11 also states emphatically, not once but several times, that this is a covenant made by God and it is an 'everlasting covenant'. This repetition prevents us from interpreting the word 'everlasting' to mean 'time lasting' or 'for a season'.

The exact words are:

Remember the wonders he has done,
his miracles, and the judgments he pronounced,
you his servants, the descendants of Abraham,
his chosen ones, the children of Jacob.
He is the LORD our God;
his judgments are in all the earth.
He remembers his covenant forever,
the promise he made, for a thousand generations,
the covenant he made with Abraham,
the oath he swore to Isaac.
He confirmed it to Jacob as a decree,
to Israel as an everlasting covenant:
'To you I will give the land of Canaan
as the portion you will inherit'.
(Ps. 105:5-11)

So here the Psalmist points us not once but five times to 'his marvellous works' and to a covenant. The covenant is not simply to Abraham but to his seed, including Isaac and Jacob, *and* to a thousand generations. In biblical terminology, a generation is usually counted as forty years and so a thousand generations, by implication, would be forty thousand years.

Let us return to our central question: 'What made the people of Israel significant in the first place?' They say that everyone aspires to fifteen minutes of fame. So let us re-bundle the question and personalise it. What makes *you* or *me* so significant in the first place? Consider for a moment. Why are we significant in the grand scheme of things? Here we are in a world that is larger than we can comprehend or measure on our own in one lifetime; a universe that makes this world look like a golf ball by comparison (and even that is being generous). Yet here are little old you and me, reading this because God chose us.

Why did he choose us? There is only one explanation. He chose us because he chose us, and he loves us because he loves us. Don't ask why, but he just does. And we have a responsibility and a calling as Christians to reflect Christ to our fellow humankind.

Israel has a similar responsibility towards all of the other nations. Israel was hand-picked by God to be his representative nation on earth. Why? Good question. In his providence, wisdom, election and eternal purpose he needed a vehicle through which the Messiah would come and the vehicle he chose was Israel.

He chose you to be a vehicle amongst your peers. He chose

Israel to be a vehicle amongst its peers (nations).

How remarkable! That means that your life on a personal level is a microcosm reflected in all that Israel goes through on a national level. We face trials and tribulations because we are chosen as sons of the Living God, adopted into his family in spite of all of our rebellion and evasiveness. Israel on the international stage, in exactly the same way, is acting nationally as we have been known to act personally. However, she will one day come home to her Father's house.

Let me give one other illustration from the familiar story which Jesus told about the prodigal son. A younger brother asks for his inheritance and leaves home to squander all of his money. He returns penniless and starving to the unexpected forgiveness of his loving father. The elder brother, who remained at home, is then incensed by the party thrown to celebrate the younger's return.

On a personal level, this is a story about the Father reaching out and welcoming us back home, even after we have rebelled and done our own thing. Imagine that in this case, Israel is the younger brother. The older brother, who is jealous upon the return of the younger brother, might be compared with the church.[3] Why are you and I not rejoicing at the return in prospect of our brother into the house of God? Are we upset that there is a party happening for Israel's return? Let us stop for a minute and rejoice that, because God had every right to save us, he also has every right to watch over and ultimately save Israel.

Israel is found in Genesis and in Revelation. As a Jewish book, the Bible traces the redemption story which is centred upon a Jewish Saviour. However, this redemption will not be fully realised until the prodigal son returns home.

Won't you join in making this a reality and pray for the peace of Jerusalem?

> May those who love you be secure …
> For the sake of my family and friends,
> I will say, 'Peace be within you.'
> For the sake of the house of the Lord our God,
> I will seek your prosperity.
> (Ps. 122:6-9)

What made the people of Israel significant can be summed up simply. It is God who made them significant and in that rests the key to one of creation's greatest mysteries.

> For you are a people holy to the Lord your God. The Lord your God has chosen you out of all the peoples on the face of the earth to be his people, his treasured possession. The Lord did not set his affection on you and choose you because you were more numerous than other peoples, for you were the fewest of all peoples. But it was because the Lord loved you and kept the oath he swore to your ancestors that he brought you out with a mighty hand and redeemed you from the land of slavery, from the power of Pharaoh king of Egypt. Know therefore that the Lord your God is God; he is the faithful God, keeping his covenant of love to a thousand generations of those who love him and keep his commandments. (Deut. 7:6-9)

End Notes

1. A 'covenant' (*diatheke* in Greek, *berith* in Hebrew) is a commitment which is so strong that it becomes a defining part of the identity of the one who makes it. A covenant can be unilateral, made by one party, or it can be bilateral, involving the commitments of two parties as is, for example, the case in a marriage covenant. Unlike a 'contract' (*suntheke* in Greek), which bases its provisions upon the ongoing fulfilment or non-fulfilment of certain conditions, a covenant is therefore always theoretically unconditional and unbreakable. (See e.g. J.B. Torrance (1970); John Murray (1953)).

2. 'Abram' means 'exalted father'. God later named him 'Abraham' (Gen. 17:5), which means 'father of many'.

3. This is not to suggest that it is appropriate to identify Israel exclusively with the younger brother in Jesus' parable, any more than that the church can be identified exclusively with the older brother. It is important to recognise that, interpreting the parable in this manner, the roles might easily be inverted. Christian antisemitism across the ages involves a denial of Jesus Christ which is at least equivalent to any alleged rejection of Messiah by the Jewish people themselves.

2. What Role Does the Promised Land Play for the People of Israel?

BY JACOB VINCE

> That God does not go back upon his distinctive covenant with Israel or change his mind about his special gifts to Israel or revoke his calling of Israel for universal mission, is central not only to the message of the Old Testament but to the message of the New Testament as well.
>
> T.F. Torrance (Theologian)

The Land of Israel was a gift promised to Abraham, Isaac and Jacob and their descendants in the Old Testament (Tanakh). The people received the land after the Exodus from Egypt and it served two unambiguous purposes: it was a visible manifestation confirming God's faithfulness to them, and it provided them with a place in which they could live as a nation called by God to be his people and a blessing to all people – ' … a land flowing with milk and honey' (Ex. 3:8).

Far less clear is what Jesus and his early followers thought of the land since none of the New Testament authors address this question directly. Even this apparent silence, if silence it is, can be interpreted in two ways: Does it provide confirmation that the ongoing significance of the land is assumed and can be inferred? Was it unnecessary to consider the land because it was a temporary gift which retained only its historical, illustrative value? Space here permits only a brief answer based on four key examples of what Stephen, Paul, the writer to the Hebrews, and finally, Jesus, in discussion with his disciples, had to say when speaking about the land.

That the land was significant in Scripture before the time of Jesus is unambiguously clear, so what we are looking for here is whether or not we detect any adjustment to their expectations about the land or their understanding of its present and/or continuing role for the people of Israel.

Stephen's Speech

In the early church, Stephen was to be the first martyr. In his defence before the Sanhedrin he recounts God's dealings with Israel, focussing upon the land promise and its physical outworking. He begins with the appearing of the God of Glory to, '*our* [Stephen and the Sanhedrin's] father Abraham' and the God of Glory's appearance to Abraham, 'while he was still in Mesopotamia' (Acts 7:2). '"Leave your country and your people," God said, "and go to *the land* I will show you"' (Acts 7:3).

Abraham did as he was instructed and following a brief period in Haran, eventually arrived in *the land*, as Stephen puts it, 'where *you* [the Sanhedrin] are now living' (Acts 7:4). Stephen correctly notes that God gave Abraham, himself, 'no inheritance here' (the land where you [the Sanhedrin] are now living), in fact not even a '*foot of ground*' (Acts 7:5). Nonetheless, or as Stephen says, '*But*, God promised him [Abraham] that he and *his descendants after him* would *possess the land*, even though at that time Abraham had *no child*' (Acts 7:5).

Physical possession necessitated the requirement of having a physical child, otherwise why did Stephen mention that Abraham had no child? First of all, the land was a provision which was to meet the needs of the people God was calling. Without the promised descendants and the land in which to live, it would not have been possible for Israel to be established as God's chosen nation: a great nation through which he would bless the world (Gen. 12:2-3).

Stephen then continues by recalling the manner in which God spoke his promise, 'God spoke to him [Abraham] in this way, "Your descendants will be strangers in a country that is *not their own*, and they will be enslaved and mistreated four hundred years"' (Acts 7:6).

The implication here is that if there is a country that is *not* their own, there is a country that *is* their own!

Mindful that Abraham had descendants through his first son, Ishmael, and Isaac through Esau, Abraham's descendants referred to earlier are clearly shown as coming through the line of Isaac and more particularly through Jacob. These sons of Jacob are otherwise described as *the tribes of Israel*, and it is clearly to *these* that God was referring when he spoke his promise to Abraham, because only *these* descendants went down to Egypt where they were, 'enslaved and mistreated for four hundred years' (Acts 7:6). This did not happen to Esau's or Ishmael's descendants.

After the period in Egypt, Stephen describes how the 'time

drew near for God to *fulfil* his promise to Abraham' (Acts 7:17). What was this promise? That, 'he and his descendants after him would possess *the land*' (Acts 7:5). This was to be processed through Moses and carried out under Joshua. The land was to be a provision, as well as a primary manifestation of God's faithfulness to his people.

Stephen continues by describing how Joshua brought the tabernacle of the testimony 'with them when they took *the land* from the nations *God* drove out before them' (Acts 7:45). This aspect of God's involvement (notice Stephen states that it was *God* who drove the nations out before them) was key to fulfilment of the *promise* made by God that they would possess the land.

Paul's Proclamation

The same point is also later reiterated by the apostle Paul in his proclamation at Pisidian Antioch, 'he [*God*] overthrew seven nations in Canaan, *giving* their land to *his* people as *their* inheritance' (Acts 13:19). Whilst we are now well in the time of the early church, there is no hint here whatsoever that this land is no longer *their* (his people's) inheritance.

It is interesting to note that Paul, as a later apostle, and Stephen, as a newly appointed deacon, both chose to detail this period of Israel's history in their defence and proclamation of the gospel. There is no question that the main emphasis of Paul's preaching was the good news of eternal salvation. Clearly the land was only part of a much bigger picture for Paul and indeed Stephen, as we would expect it to be for the church today. Nevertheless, in his discourse Paul definitively recognises God's giving of the land to the people of Israel in the time of Joshua (Acts 13:17-20).

What is more, Paul would not have wasted words stating such matters without his wishing to attach to them due importance, *indeed even ongoing importance*, in the bringing of the message of salvation.

Retaining the connection of this message to its roots was certainly important for Paul. The response to the message by his audience was also marked in that, 'many of the Jews and devout converts to Judaism followed Paul and Barnabas, who talked with them and urged them to continue in the grace of God' (Acts 13:43).

For Paul, the land was the companion and confirmation of the gospel, particularly among the Jewish people he addressed, because it formed part of the foundation of God's relationship with Israel. The land was equally a part both of the identity of the people and of God's identity since he was the 'God of the *people of Israel*' (Acts 13:17) who gave it to them. The opposite suggestion, that the land was no longer important, would therefore have amounted to severing the gospel completely from Israel's history.

Hebrews' Heroes

The identification between Israel, God and the land can be clearly seen in another passage that similarly discusses the matter of the promised land in detail. Hebrews chapter 11 famously records the exercise of faith by those who are called, 'a great cloud of witnesses' (Heb. 12:1). Whilst *faith* is the primary focus of the passage, at the same time it provides an insight into the writer's thinking with regard to the *land* of Israel:

> By faith Abraham, when called to go to a place he would later receive as his inheritance, obeyed and went, even though he did not know where he was going. By faith he made his home in the *promised* land like a stranger in a foreign country; he lived in tents as did Isaac and Jacob, who were heirs with him of *the same promise*. (Heb. 11:8-9)

The passage also goes on to show that Abraham 'was looking forward to the city with foundations, whose architect and builder is God' (Heb. 11:10). However, we see no suggestion here that 'heavenly' promises and 'earthly' promises are opposed to one another, or held to be mutually exclusive. On the contrary, the expectation of a 'heavenly' city, a heavenly Jerusalem, appears to be based upon the 'earthly' one: that there is a land promised to Abraham, through the family line of his descendants. It describes the status of these descendants as being *like* a stranger, with the implication that their actual status was not that of a stranger but rather of those to whom *the promise of the land* had been given. In exercising faith towards the promise being outworked physically, Abraham, beyond all natural possibilities (i.e. miraculously), 'was enabled to become a father because he considered him faithful who had made *the promise*' (Heb. 11:11).

The passage then describes Abraham's numerous descendants who exercised faith but did not receive the things promised (Heb. 11:13). The same is true of Isaac,

Jacob and Joseph, the later of whom demonstrated his belief in the eventual exodus of the Israelites from Egypt by giving instructions about his bones one day being buried back in the promised land (Heb. 11:22). This detail all alludes to the earlier biblical record of 'the land promised on oath' to Joseph's father, grandfather and great-grandfather, 'Abraham, Isaac and Jacob' (Gen. 50:24-25).

We find the other descendants of the patriarchs coming into the picture and gaining what was promised, 'Gideon, Barak, Samson, Jephthah, David, Samuel and the prophets, who through faith conquered kingdoms, administered justice, and *gained what was promised*' (Heb. 11:32-33).

Undoubtedly, the ultimate reward of the faith of this multitude was something better and more lasting than a land or country in this life, even the land of Israel, but rather that of the heavenly dimension. Nonetheless, the pursuit by faith of *the land promised by God* is still most highly commended and so it would be only appropriate to interpret the inheritance of the land itself is an outworking of faith too.

Luke's Logistics

In what the Bible calls the 'last days', the last two thousand years or so (Acts 2:16-21 quoting Joel 2:28-32) God has spoken through his Son (Heb. 1:1-3). That which God spoke through his Son was entrusted to the apostles to write down for us. So what did the apostles record about Jesus' life and what he said concerning the land of Israel?

There are two clear instances where Jesus specifically responds to the disciples' understanding concerning the restoration of the kingdom to Israel. Both come after Jesus' resurrection.

The first immediately follows it, on the road to Emmaus, 'We had hoped that he was the one who was going to redeem Israel' (Luke 24:19-21). The second is the last recorded conversation of the apostles with Jesus before he ascended, 'Lord, are you at this time going to restore the kingdom to Israel?' (Acts 1:6).

The first occurs *before* Jesus had revealed his risen self, but the second occurs *after* Jesus' explanation on the road to Emmaus as to what was said in the Scriptures concerning himself (Luke 24:27), a meeting with a larger number of his disciples where Jesus opened their minds so they could understand the Scriptures (Luke 24:45), and *after* Jesus had appeared to his disciples over a period of forty days, speaking to them about the kingdom of God (Acts 1:3).

So how does Jesus respond to these respective questions of the disciples?

In the first conversation, Jesus responds with the words, 'How foolish you are, and how slow to believe *all* that the prophets have spoken!' (Luke 24:25).

Whilst it is correct that Jesus refers to these disciples as foolish and slow of heart to believe, he does not explicitly dismiss their hope in the redemption of Israel. Jesus' comment is in relation to their believing *all* that the prophets had written. The implication is that they believed *some* though not *all*. In other words, they had arguably got it right about the redemption of Israel, if not the timing, as we will see, but had missed the *entirety* of what the prophets told, in particular, about *Jesus* in the Scriptures. Such a suggestion is supported by the words Jesus uses, referring to what the Scriptures say, specifically, 'concerning *himself*' (Luke 24:27).

If we go back briefly to Jesus' earlier prediction about his suffering and death we see the same thing paralleled:

Jesus took the twelve aside and told them, 'We are going up to Jerusalem, and *everything* that is written by the prophets *about the Son of Man* will be fulfilled. He will be delivered over to the Gentiles. They will mock him, insult him and spit on him; they will flog him and kill him. On the third day he will rise again.' The disciples did not understand any of this. Its meaning was hidden from them, and they did not know what he was talking about. (Luke 18:31-34)

If Jesus was referring in Luke 24 to everything written by the prophets about *him* that would be fulfilled, it would seem unlikely that Jesus advocated rejecting what the prophets wrote about the restoration of the kingdom to Israel. This would actually contradict his teaching that the disciples needed to *believe* what the prophets had written.

In the second conversation the disciples ask a question about timing, 'Lord, are you at *this time* going to restore the kingdom to Israel?' (Acts 1:6), *when* not *whether*. Jesus, in response, does not question the assumption as to whether the kingdom would be restored to Israel but rather answers with regard to the matter of timing, by saying, 'It is not for you to know the times or dates God has set' (Acts 1:7).[4]

So on both occasions the implication is that Israel as a

land remained important, but *in addition* to, as opposed to being made redundant by, the purpose of God in sending his Son, Jesus.

There is a common message which recurs in each of these New Testament passages: that God, who makes promises, keeps them. The promises he makes about physical matters he keeps in physical terms, so that through them we can also know that the promises he makes about spiritual matters he does and will also keep. The promised land is important because God uses it to demonstrate his faithfulness for all time and to all people who come to him by faith, including the Jewish people and everyone who has been and ever will be part of the church.

End Notes

4. There is a widely held view that Jesus' words here demonstrate the disciples' overall lack of understanding that the kingdom of God is not of this world (e.g. John 18:36); that they were mistakenly clinging to the hope of a restored political kingdom for Israel. It is certainly true, as we have seen, that the kingdom which Jesus proclaimed is far more than a political kingdom. This explains Jesus' answer redirecting their attention to the coming of the Holy Spirit. Nevertheless, Jesus had an opportunity here to correct his disciples' world view unambiguously and he did not take it. Therefore, the burden of proof remains firmly with the view that the disciples were clinging to an expired promise.

3. Why Were the People Exiled?

By David Noakes

It is high time for Christians to interpret unfulfilled prophecy by the light of prophecy already fulfilled. The curses on the Jews were brought to pass literally; so also will be the blessings. The scattering was literal; so also will be the gathering. The pulling down of Zion was literal; so also will be the building up. The rejection of Israel was literal; so also will be the restoration.

J.C. Ryle (First Bishop of Liverpool, 1880-1900)

If you do not carefully follow all the words of this law, which are written in this book, and do not revere this glorious and awesome name – the LORD your God – the LORD will send fearful plagues on you and your descendants, harsh and prolonged disasters, and severe and lingering illnesses. (Deut. 28:58-59)

Just as it pleased the LORD to make you prosper and increase in number, so it will please him to ruin and destroy you. You will be uprooted from the land you are entering to possess. Then the LORD will scatter you among all nations, from one end of the earth to the other. (Deut. 28:63-64)

Through Moses it was consistently made clear by God to the chosen people, the descendants of Jacob, that his requirements of them were simple, but absolute: they were commanded to keep the Law given at Sinai in the form of the Ten Commandments. Above all, they were to worship the LORD, the one true God, and none other; as Jesus later reaffirmed, the first and greatest commandment was to 'love the Lord your God with all your heart and with all your soul and with all your mind' (Matt. 22:37 quoting Deut. 6:5).

The Teacher, in Ecclesiastes, summarises the requirements of his people towards God succinctly, 'Fear God and keep his commandments, for this is the duty of all mankind' (Eccl. 12:13). Moses had warned them:

> See, I set before you today life and prosperity, death and destruction. For I command you today to love the LORD your God, to walk in obedience to him, and to keep his commands, decrees and laws; then you will live and increase, and the LORD your God will bless you in the land you are entering to possess. But if your heart turns away and you are not obedient, and if you are drawn away to bow down to other gods and worship them, I declare to you this day that you will certainly be destroyed. You will not live long in the land you are crossing the Jordan to enter and possess. (Deut. 30:15-18)

The matter had thus been made plain to the children of Israel before ever they crossed the Jordan to take possession of the land of Canaan. Although the land had been promised by the unilateral and unconditional covenant of God to Abraham and his descendants as an everlasting possession (Gen. 15:7-21, 17:8) and reaffirmed to Isaac and to Jacob in turn (Gen. 26:2-3, 28:13, 35:12; Ps. 105:7-11), nevertheless, although the right of possession of the land was and remains irrevocable, the right to occupy it was not unconditional. Under the Mosaic covenant, the right of continued occupation was dependent upon obedience to the command to worship God and no other, and to demonstrate reverence towards him by obeying the laws he had given at Sinai.

The requirement was simple, but to meet that requirement would prove impossible, because of the inherent tendency towards rebellion and disobedience which is characteristic of our fallen, fleshly nature – the same problem which the apostle Paul agonises over in Romans chapter 7, the battle between the desires of the spirit to obey and the urge of the flesh towards self-gratification and disobedience. Moses was all too well aware that despite the promises of the blessings, which would result from obedience and the warnings of the consequences of disobedience, the nation of Israel would nevertheless rebel and ultimately be banished into exile from the land, as he makes plain through his words to the people in Deuteronomy 29:22 – 30:1-6. He knew it to be inevitable – not a matter of 'if', but of 'when' (Deut. 30:1-2).

The whole history of the nation of Israel, Jacob's descendants, as recorded in the pages of the Bible, has followed the same pattern right down to the restoration of the sovereign State of Israel in May 1948. It is a long story of fluctuation between periods of obedience and blessing, and periods of steadily increasing rebellion against God and disobedience to his commandments.

The history of Israel is a long saga of God's astonishing patience and forbearance with his chosen nation whom he loves with an everlasting love (Jer. 31:3); of his warnings to them through the prophets, and his pleadings with them to repent and not to bring down upon themselves the judgment of being first oppressed by their enemies and finally sent into exile. To banish his people from the land he had given them was the last resort, which he avoided for as long as possible until finally they had overstepped the mark and he 'removed them from his presence, as he had warned through all his servants the prophets' (2 Kings 17:23).

Jeremiah underlines the key factors which brought about the exile of first the northern kingdom of Israel, and later the southern kingdom of Judah, 'My people have committed two sins: they have forsaken me, the spring of living water, and have dug their own cisterns, broken cisterns that cannot hold water' (Jer. 2:13).

The breaking of all the other commandments is rooted in the breaking of the first commandment; when God's people turn away from worship and reverence towards him, the result is always to seek security and satisfaction in substitutes, which cannot satisfy, and seduce them into further ways of lawlessness. Israel's fundamental sin is that of rejecting God's right to rule over his people and receive their worship and obedience – the same root sin which is common to all descendants of Adam.

The prophets warned the nation again and again, pleading

for repentance from idolatry and a return to the worship of God, but almost invariably in vain, and at the cost of utter hatred against themselves for bringing the unwanted message. They were men who cared deeply, both for God and for his rebellious people, 'My eyes fail from weeping … because my people are destroyed' says Jeremiah (Lam. 2:11); yet he had also cried out concerning himself, 'Alas, my mother, that you gave me birth, a man with whom the whole land strives and contends … everyone curses me' (Jer. 15:10).

Following the division of the kingdom into two as judgment upon Solomon's turning away from God, Jeroboam had instituted in the northern kingdom of Israel the idolatry of the worship of two golden calves. This sin continued without repentance for nearly two centuries, resulting finally in the exile of the northern kingdom to Assyria in 721 BC, from which they never returned.

The southern kingdom of Judah was exiled to Babylon in 586 BC for a period of 70 years, but a remnant then returned to rebuild Jerusalem and the temple. Yet despite the experience of one banishment into exile, Judah's sin of rejecting God as King persisted. Overt idol-worship had ceased, but no wholehearted return to the ways of the LORD followed, as is evidenced, for instance, by the shout of one small group of Jews that 'we have no king but *Caesar*' (John 19:15), a clear rejection of God's command through Moses, 'Be sure to appoint over you a king the LORD your God chooses … Do not place a foreigner over you, one who is not an Israelite' (Deut. 17:15). In anguish, Jesus had prophesied that another exile would take place:

'Jerusalem, Jerusalem ... how often I have longed to gather your children together, as a hen gathers her chicks under her wings, and you were not willing. Look, your house is left to you desolate. For I tell you, you will not see me again until you say, "Blessed is he who comes in the name of the Lord." (Matt. 23:37-39; see also Luke 21:6)

Ironically, it was *Caesar's* army which destroyed Jerusalem in 70 AD after a rebellion. A second failed rebellion took place against the Romans in 132 AD led by a false 'messiah' called Bar Kokhba, a century after Jesus' death and resurrection. In response, the Romans exiled the vast majority of the people from the land and renamed it 'Palestine' (after Israel's old enemies, the 'Philistines') as a final insult. The second exile, which was to last for almost 1900 years, began.

4. Why Did the People Return?

By Adam Raffell

May the Spirit grant the Christian consciousness to be convulsed ... I have in mind the kind of tremors Zionism has created in Judaism for more than a hundred years but that have barely registered any aftershocks in Christianity. This holds Christians in a fatal historical imbalance and inequality over against the history of Israel.

Friedrich-Wilhelm Marquardt (Theologian)

When all these blessings and curses I have set before you come on you and you take them to heart wherever the LORD your God disperses you among the nations, and when you and your children return to the LORD your God and obey him with all your heart and with all your soul according to everything I command you today, then the LORD your God will restore your fortunes and have compassion on you and gather you again from all the nations where he scattered you. Even if you have been banished to the most distant land under the heavens, from there the LORD your God will gather you and bring you back. He will bring you to the land that belonged to your ancestors, and you will take possession of it. He will make you more prosperous and numerous than your ancestors. The LORD your God will circumcise your hearts and the hearts of your descendants, so that you may love him with all your heart and with all your soul, and live. (Deut. 30:1-6)

The people were on the brink of entering the promised land. As the book of Deuteronomy approached its climax with Joshua about to be named as Moses' successor, something slightly odd happened: God promised the people a return from exile. The people had not even entered the land! What was going on?

What these verses tell us is that when the inevitable happens – Israel failed to live as God instructed and consequently suffered exile – God promised to do something about it. He would bring them back! We also see that this return depends upon the people returning to God with all their heart and soul, but the passage is even more precise. God promised to change or 'circumcise' the hearts of his people so that they could love him as they should. That, in essence, is the message of the cross which the Christian gospel invites each of us to accept: in Jesus Christ, God has forgiven – 'carried away' from each one of us – our own wrongdoing and rebellion and has clothed us with his own righteous obedience. Jesus offered his own true worship to our heavenly Father in our place. A parallel message rings in the ears of God's people here as they enter the land. It is God's eternal promise of a 'nevertheless'. When the people have been exiled, *nevertheless*, God promised from the outset to implement an initiative which would *both* change their hearts *and* bring them back to the land.

There is no limit given. No matter how far away they go; however long they are gone; however the people have rebelled and lost their way, the promise remains. This passage is especially significant because it provides the framework for interpreting all of the many words concerning exile and return which are later spoken through the prophets. Exile implies return.

At this moment, God wonderfully demonstrated that the journey upon which he has brought his people – the covenant with Abraham, Isaac and Jacob promising the land of Canaan to their descendants, the covenant at Sinai under Moses telling the people how they must live – did not culminate in a contractual relationship. Their future return was not ultimately conditional or contingent upon their obedience, although the latter would always be required. God's covenants[5] remain from beginning to end an initiative of divine grace.

The question of whether obedience might still be expected to precede a return of Jewish people to Israel is, in principle, a legitimate one. With that acknowledgement, however, a word of caution: as Christians, we simply cannot presume to judge the extent to which the Jewish people today are obedient to God or to place limitations upon a covenant relationship which he so emphatically established. This is especially the case in the light of our faith that one Jewish man has already offered obedience on behalf of the people of Israel (and all people) with all his heart and soul, once for all – Jesus Christ! As Paul explained, 'For just as through the disobedience of the one man the many were made sinners, so also through the

obedience of the one man the many will be made righteous'
(Rom. 5:19).

Christ's wholehearted obedience completed and perfected
Israel's obedience as a nation, on their behalf, irrespective
of whether or not individual Jewish people have received
him. In this sense, therefore, it is possible to consider any
subsequent return of the Jewish people to the land of promise
to be in accordance with the words of Deuteronomy 30 and
its insistence that Israel's return would be accompanied by
their obedience.

So we know that the Jewish people returned to the land in
the past because God promised that they would. However, if
that is the case today too, then for what purpose is he bringing
them back? At first appearance a Christian could be forgiven
for thinking that after the time of Christ this promise appears
rather arbitrary: apart from everything else God is doing in
the world through the church, for some unknown reason he
has tied himself to keeping what is surely now an outdated
promise concerning a piece of real estate for one group of
people in the Middle East! What is that when compared with
the Christian hope of eternal life with God ruling the whole
earth as King?

Let's take a moment to examine just one example from
the book of Isaiah, chapter 11, in which we can observe an
inseparable association between Israel's restoration from exile
and God ultimately establishing his rule over the whole earth.
This chapter begins:

A shoot will come up from the stump of Jesse;
from his roots a Branch will bear fruit.
The Spirit of the LORD will rest on him ...
and he will delight in the fear of the LORD.
(Isa. 11:1-3)

Jesse was the father of King David, and so these verses promise a descendant of David's line. The kings of Israel were the Lord's 'anointed' (chosen by God), and the Hebrew word for this is *meshiach* ('messiah' or 'christ'). So this is a reference to a messiah.

The passage continues, 'The wolf will live with the lamb, the leopard will lie down with the goat, the calf and the lion and the yearling together; and a little child will lead them' (Isa. 11:6). And then, 'They will neither harm nor destroy on all my holy mountain, for the earth will be filled with the knowledge of the LORD as the waters cover the sea' (Isa. 11:9).

The meaning of this messiah is defined here that he is to bring about Isaiah's poetically described age of universal peace: the kingdom of God – God's rule over all of the earth.

In that day the Root of Jesse will stand as a banner for the peoples; the nations will rally to him, and his resting place will be glorious. In that day the Lord will reach out his hand a second time to reclaim the surviving remnant of his people ...
He will raise a banner for the nations
and gather the exiles of Israel;
he will assemble the scattered people of Judah
from the four quarters of the earth. (Isa. 11:10-12)

Next, God is described as reaching out to re-gather the exiled people of Israel. According to Isaiah here, the return of the people not only signifies the coming of the kingdom of God, but it is part of it. The Davidic King – this Root of Jesse messiah-figure who reigns over Israel – is also the one who extends his kingdom to the Gentiles. In other words, Israel's re-gathering and restoration is presented as being itself part of the good news of the kingdom of God, which is being given in Christ for all people.

In summary, therefore, we have identified two main reasons why the Jewish people returned, which are in essence really the same reason. Firstly, Deuteronomy 30 explains that the restoration of the Jewish people would take place from wherever they have been exiled. Israel's return to the home which he provided for them confirms God's covenant faithfulness with the Jewish people. Secondly, Isaiah 11 shows us that the hope of Messiah – the ruler of Israel and the one who reaches out to all nations – can never be divorced from the return of the people of Israel, and vice versa. Although the specific relationship between Israel's return and Messiah is not precisely defined here, what is clear is that we cannot expect one without the other. Israel's return cannot be complete without Messiah and a messiah who does not ultimately facilitate a return for the Jewish people would not be the Messiah of the Jewish people (or, therefore, 'Messiah' in any sense at all). Simply put, if we have faith in Messiah and the establishment of God's kingdom then it follows that the promise of return for the Jewish people is an ongoing promise because Messiah is Israel's king. These two reasons ultimately boil down to one single reason – namely, that God promised he would. This is why each time the Jewish people have been exiled, God has always brought them back.

End Notes

5. I refer here to God's covenants collectively – Creation, Noahic, Abrahamic, Mosaic, Davidic, and 'New' – assuming perpetuity, continuity and mutual interdependence between them.

5. WHO IS JESUS?

BY ADAM RAFFELL

> Israel is nothing apart from Jesus Christ; but we also have to say that Jesus Christ would not be Jesus Christ apart from Israel. So first of all we must look for a moment at this Israel, in order to be able really to look at Jesus Christ.
> Karl Barth (Theologian)

This question is really the preeminent question. It's the question which will never go away. It is the most important question to be answered by each and every human being who has ever lived and ever will live, but it is also a question which cannot be adequately answered without reference to the people of Israel, which is my purpose in asking it.

Mark's Gospel opens with his answer, 'The beginning of the good news about Jesus Christ the Son of God' (Mark 1:1). By far the clearest and most fundamental claim made about Jesus in all of the Gospels and throughout the New Testament is this one, that he is the 'Christ' (Hebrew, *Meshiach* – anglicised 'Messiah' – 'anointed one'). Israel's kings (civic leaders) and priests (religious leaders and intercessors) were literally anointed with oil to mark their having been chosen or elected by God for a role of responsibility. This signified that they were being made holy ('set apart') by God in order to be able to fulfil that role and serve his people through it. To call Jesus 'Christ' therefore means to say that he was God's 'chosen one', like a king or priest of Israel. Was Jesus a priest or a king, or called to be something else altogether? Who is this 'Christ'?

No one answer is quite enough, so we need to do a little digging. We get an early glimpse of Jesus when his birth is announced by an angel to his mother, Mary:

> 'Do not be afraid, Mary, you have found favour with God. You will conceive and give birth to a son, and you are to call him Jesus. He will be great and will be called the Son of the Most High. The Lord God will give him the throne of his father David, and he will reign over Jacob's descendants for ever; his kingdom will never end.'
> (Luke 1:30-33)

Joseph, who was betrothed to Mary when she became pregnant, also received confirmation from 'an angel of the Lord' in a dream:

> 'Joseph son of David, do not be afraid to take Mary home as your wife, because what is conceived in her is from the Holy Spirit. She will give birth to a son, and you are to give him the name Jesus, because he will save his people from their sins.' (Matt. 1:20-21).

Already a multifaceted picture of Jesus' identity had begun

to take shape in these announcements: he is born of Davidic descent; he is also the Son of the Lord Most High and the Ruler of Israel ('the house of Jacob'). Both Matthew and Luke record that Jesus was born to Mary while she was still a virgin and that she was impregnated by the Holy Spirit of God. This gives rise to a concept called the 'incarnation': that Jesus is literally, physically and historically the Son of the living God – God himself born as a human being.

John's Gospel, with painstaking precision, explains further, 'In the beginning was the Word, and the Word was with God, and the Word was God. He was with God in the beginning' (John 1:1-2), and with Jesus' birth, 'The Word became flesh and made his dwelling among us. We have seen his glory, the glory of the one and only Son, who came from the Father, full of grace and truth' (John 1:14). This is the starting premise of Christian faith.

The name, 'Jesus' (the Greek rendering of *Yeshua* – or 'Joshua' as we would pronounce it in English), means 'the LORD saves'. This Jesus, 'Joshua', is God's Saviour; God himself saving the world from sin and establishing his eternal reign or kingdom.

Calling Jesus *a* Christ, or even *the* Christ, does not itself actually mean 'God' at all. Rather, what is truly groundbreaking about Jesus in the accounts of the Gospels and the New Testament is that Jesus' anointing, what it means to call him 'Christ', *is explained in terms of* him being the Word of God made flesh. The good news is that the one who God anoints, chooses or elects, is God *himself.*[6] The LORD God of Israel chooses to invest himself in humankind and to call them *his* people, eternally, becoming a man and an Israelite in order to perfect Israel from within as their servant-king and representative from David's line. And God's attitude towards Israel essentially demonstrates his attitude towards every person.

Jesus could represent Israel because he was, through and through, a Jewish man. He observed the instructions of the Torah (Genesis to Deuteronomy). He was circumcised a Jewish child and immersed in the water of the river Jordan by John the Baptist in an act which at that time was a Jewish practice. In fact, most of what he did took place in the land of Israel: he walked beside the Sea of Galilee; calmed a storm; cursed a fig tree so that it withered; raised a young girl and his friend, Lazarus, from death. He taught many thousands as a Rabbi of Israel and discipled twelve apostles. He went up to Jerusalem for the feasts and worshipped in the house of the Lord (the 'temple'). He was betrayed and then crucified there under its Roman occupiers and was sealed in a tomb. However, he rose from the dead three days later and was seen by more than five hundred people (1 Cor. 15:6) before he ascended into heaven with the promise that he will one day return to rule the whole world.

It is only in retrospect, with the coming of Jesus and the witness of the Gospels, that the various promises of the Tanakh (Old Testament), some of which were promises to be carried out by God himself, others by distinctive priestly or kingly messiahs, might be seen to be interwoven: part of one divine saving work which encompasses all of them at once. This was a brand new development; something quite unexpected but truly wonderful.

By calling Jesus 'Christ', God re-endorsed and extended his existing relationship with the people of Israel. Jesus is the confirmation of all of his promises to them and also his promises to the world through them – as he had said to Abraham right at the beginning, 'And all peoples on earth will be blessed through you' (Gen. 12:3). By acknowledging himself as 'Christ', Jesus consciously bound himself to confirming God's promises, as their true and final instigator. As Paul explains in his second letter to a church in the ancient city of Corinth:

> But as surely as God is faithful, our message to you is not 'Yes' and 'No.' For the Son of God, Jesus Christ, who was preached among you by us – by me and Silas and Timothy – was not 'Yes' and 'No,' but in him it has always been 'Yes.' For no matter how many promises God has made, they are 'Yes' in Christ. And so through him the 'Amen' is spoken by us to the glory of God. (2 Cor. 1:18-20)

These words summarise perfectly who Jesus is. Jesus is God's 'Yes' to Israel and also his 'Yes' to all of the people of the world – you and me. Jesus, who died on the cross at Calvary, rejected by human beings, took upon himself God's 'No' to Israel's sins and also to each of our own sins. Through his taking God's 'No' to us, as we are, upon himself we can instead know God's 'Yes' to us: his unconditional decision to be with us now and forever. His resurrection is a final, decisive and resounding 'Yes' to Israel's (and our own) prayers to receive

God's mercy upon each of our lives.

Jesus is God's 'Yes' to Israel's (and our own) prayers to be holy people, living lives of unreserved obedience to God's word – what the Jewish people call 'Torah' (although what this obedience involves from a Gentile is somewhat different). He is the 'Yes' to God's promises for Israel concerning the covenantal gift of the land and of return from exile to the land, just as he is the 'Yes' to God's promise to grant people from all nations, you and me, full membership in the house of Israel. We become sons and daughters of Abraham in Christ. Jesus is ultimately God's 'Yes' to the hope of eternal life in the kingdom of God for Jews and for Gentiles, now and forevermore. Words on a page alone cannot do this justice!

End Notes

6. An allusion to Karl Barth's insight that Jesus is the subject and object of election: both the *electing* God and the one *elected* man (see *Church Dogmatics*, II.2 p95ff.).

6. Did the Disciples Stop Being 'Jews'?

Jewish Continuity in Messiah

By Jonathan Allen

> ... how is it possible for a Jewish person to remain placid when visiting a Christian place of worship – listening to hymns and Bible readings which mention Israel as land or people – and then be confronted with the extraordinary transformation when his so-familiar names suddenly mean 'Gentile-believers' and 'The Church'?
>
> Johanna-Ruth Dobschiner ('Hebrew-Christian' and Holocaust survivor)

The Jewish people are not Jews because they chose to be so, but because God chose them. This has always been God's choice:

> For you are a people holy to the LORD your God. The LORD your God has chosen you out of all the peoples on the face of the earth to be his people, his treasured possession. The LORD did not set his affection on you and choose you because you were more numerous than other peoples, for you were the fewest of all peoples. But it was because the LORD loved you and kept the oath he swore to your ancestors. (Deut. 7:6-8)

God has confirmed his choice in the Jewish people through the pages of the Bible by giving them commandments that apply for all generations and for all time, using expressions such as 'throughout your generations', 'for ever and ever', 'permanent for all time':

> The Israelites are to observe the Sabbath, celebrating it for the generations to come as a lasting covenant. It will be a sign between me and the Israelites for ever, for in six days the LORD made the heavens and the earth, and on the seventh day he rested and was refreshed. (Exod. 31:16-17)

God spoke through the prophets to stress the unbreakable nature of his covenant with the descendants of Abraham, Isaac and Jacob:

> This is what the LORD says,
> he who appoints the sun
> to shine by day,
> who decrees the moon and stars
> to shine by night,
> who stirs up the sea
> so that its waves roar –
> the LORD Almighty is his name:
> 'Only if these decrees vanish from my sight,'
> declares the LORD,
> 'will Israel ever cease
> being a nation before me.'
> This is what the LORD says:

'Only if the heavens above can be measured
and the foundations of the earth below be searched out
will I reject all the descendants of Israel because of all they
have done,'
declares the Lord. (Jer. 31:35-37)

Jesus also confirmed the permanence and unalterable nature
of God's agreement with Israel:

Do not think that I have come to abolish the Law or the
Prophets; I have not come to abolish them but to fulfil
them. For truly I tell you, until heaven and earth disappear,
not the smallest letter, not the least stroke of a pen, will
by any means disappear from the Law until everything is
accomplished. (Matt. 5:17-18)

Jews who have believed and trusted in Jesus as the Messiah
of Israel remain Jews: their ancestry, their upbringing, their
calling as part of the people of Israel is a critical part of who
they are and how God wants them to be.

The apostle Paul asks:

What advantage, then, is there in being a Jew, or what value
is there in circumcision? Much in every way! First of all, the
Jews have been entrusted with the very words of God. What
if some were unfaithful? Will their unfaithfulness nullify
God's faithfulness? (Rom. 3:1-3)

As the ancient recipients, holders and maintainers of the

Hebrew Scriptures – some would say, the Greek Scriptures as well[7] – God's faithfulness and purpose preserve the Jewish people as his chosen instrument, despite their failures.

> Theirs is the adoption to sonship; theirs the divine glory, the covenants, the receiving of the law, the temple worship and the promises. Theirs are the patriarchs, and from them is traced the human ancestry of the Messiah, who is God over all, forever praised! Amen. (Rom. 9:4-5)

Notice how Paul uses the present tense here, 'theirs is', not the past, 'theirs was'. He maintains the current and ongoing stewardship of the Jewish people in these matters.

> As far as the gospel is concerned, they are enemies for your sake; but as far as election is concerned, they are loved on account of the patriarchs, for God's gifts and his call are irrevocable. (Rom. 11:28-29)

While the as yet unbelieving-in-Jesus Jewish people continue to oppose the gospel, they remain loved and called because of God's faithfulness and the promises made to the patriarchs. God's gifts and calling – as his chosen people – cannot be withdrawn or cancelled.

But does a Jew become a Christian when they come to faith in Messiah? Technically, if 'Christian' means simply 'a follower of Christ', then yes. However, 'Christian' does not imply Gentile, so Jewish believers in Messiah should not simply assimilate into the Christian church and, for all intents and purposes, disappear from Israel. Paul is very specific about calling:

> Nevertheless, each person should live as a believer in whatever situation the Lord has assigned to them, just as God has called them. This is the rule I lay down in all the churches. Was a man already circumcised when he was called? He should not become uncircumcised. Was a man uncircumcised when he was called? He should not be circumcised. Circumcision is nothing and uncircumcision is nothing. Keeping God's commands is what counts. Each person should remain in the situation they were in when God called them. (1 Cor. 7:17-20)

Jews remain Jews and Gentiles remain Gentiles, while both are equal and valued members of the body of Christ. Neither should try to adopt the status of the other; Jews should not become or behave as Gentiles and neither should Gentiles become or behave as Jews. What matters, Paul says, is keeping the commandments of God in the appropriate way for each group. This is why Paul can say, 'There is neither Jew nor Gentile, neither slave nor free, nor is there male and female, for you are all one in Christ Jesus' (Gal. 3:28).

Although one in Messiah, the separate components remain visible and identifiable. Indeed, that is the miracle of the One New Man (Eph. 2:14) – not that everyone has become a homogenised, anaemic and tasteless blend, but that despite their different cultures, languages and even physical appearances, the body of Christ works together, cares for each other and has one aim and purpose.

Jews, then, are called to retain their Jewish identity, their Jewish practice, their Jewish lifestyle, their Jewish family and friends – so far as they do not contradict Scripture – when they become believers in Jesus as Messiah. They are to continue to be the part of Israel that they are, while walking in newness of life (Rom. 6:4) and the power of the Spirit (Rom. 15:13). This was the practice of the first believers in Jerusalem, 'They devoted themselves to the apostles' teaching and to fellowship, to the breaking of bread and to prayer' (Acts 2:42).

> Every day they continued to meet together in the temple courts. They broke bread in their homes and ate together with glad and sincere hearts, praising God and enjoying the favour of all the people. (Acts 2:46-47)

They carried on worshipping in the temple, at the appointed times (see Acts 3:1), with the traditional prayers. They ate together – here, 'breaking of bread' is arguably not a reference to the taking of communion, but to the everyday Jewish practice of blessing God and breaking the bread around the table at the start of every meal – praising God, and were consequently completely accepted by the other Jews around them as well within the normal range of Jewish expression in second temple times.[8]

When Gentiles were added to the church, they too were not required to change their identity. The Jerusalem council (Acts 15) ruled that circumcision and conversion to Judaism was not required of them and stipulated only a minimal set of observance, 'To abstain from food polluted by idols, from sexual immorality, from the meat of strangled animals and from blood' (Acts 15:20).

This was to enable table fellowship and the sharing of teaching. Many scholars now think that these rules were the equivalent to the Noachide laws promulgated by Rabbinic Judaism for Gentiles today.[9] This is the physical means of bringing the Gentiles near (Eph. 2:13) so that they could share in the promises and covenants of grace (Eph. 2:12; 2:19).

Did the original, Jewish disciples stop being 'Jews'? The evidence of Scripture is that they did not and neither is there any Scriptural expectation that Jews who come to faith in Messiah today should do so either.

End Notes

7. Just as the Hebrew Scriptures were all written by Jewish people, the Greek Scriptures were also written by Jews – Luke being recognised by most scholars as a Jewish proselyte. One scholar even suggests that Luke was a priest (Rick Strellan, 2008).

8. See Daniel Boyarin (2012).

9. For example: Joseph Shulam and Hilary le Cornu (2003); Marcus Bockmuehl (2000); F.F. Bruce (1988).

7. Is Israel Still 'Israel'?

An Exploration of the Ongoing Relationship of Jews and Christians

By Alex Jacob

> The only justifiable gentile Christian 'mission to the Jews' is the reminder to the Jews of their own gracious election, and its promise for humanity. This is surely what Paul means by 'making Israel jealous' for the faith that saves (Rom. 11:14).
> Jürgen Moltman (Theologian)

Setting the Scene

The matter of how the term 'Israel' is defined and applied is one of the most important issues within Jewish-Christian relations today. For most people the term 'Israel' refers to the State of Israel, the nation formed in 1948. Yet in theological circles, the term 'Israel' is often used to convey other meanings beyond the current nation state, such as 'Jewish people', 'chosen people' and 'promised land'. Often the wider context is to do with God's redemptive purposes and God's ongoing work of election.

From the Bible, the term 'Israel' is the new name given to the patriarch Jacob after his encounter with God (Gen. 32:28). Following on from this, Jacob's sons became known as the sons of Israel (*bene Yisrael*) and the term 'Israelites' eventually came to be used to describe all of Jacob's descendants. Later still, the term was often used to describe the Jewish northern kingdom (conquered in 722 BC) as distinct from the southern kingdom of Judah.

In the Gospels, the term 'Israel' is used to refer to both the historic people of God (Matt. 2:6; Luke 4:25) and the present life of the Jewish people (Matt. 8:10; John 3:10); in this sense the term is both spiritual and ethnic. Within the Gospels, Jesus is seen as the One who will bring revelation to the Gentiles (non-Jews) and glory to the Lord's people, Israel (Luke 2:32). His disciples hoped that Jesus would be the One who would redeem Israel (Luke 24:21).

The ministry of Jesus is proclaimed largely within the context of the hope and life of Israel's calling. Jesus comes to redeem, restore and renew Israel. His ministry is a fulfilment of the hopes of the nation, the temple, the Torah and the prophets. The ministry of Jesus is declared to be the ministry of the perfect Priest, Prophet and King of Israel.

In the wider New Testament, the term 'Israel' is often interchangeable with the term 'Jew'. As the New Testament records the growth of the early church (the community of Jewish and Gentile followers of Jesus) out from the Jewish centre into the wider Gentile world, there is a major emphasis on how the church relates to Israel, how Jews and Gentiles relate to each other, and how God's purposes and Torah (Genesis to Deuteronomy) promises are to be fulfilled both within a Jewish and non-Jewish context. These questions which have pastoral, theological and evangelistic implications help shape much of Paul's writing. We see clear examples of issues stimulated by such fundamental questions in most of Paul's thirteen New Testament letters, including his letter to the Romans, especially in chapters 9-11. It is to these chapters we now turn.

Exploring the Text

In Romans 9-11, Paul declares that his love for Jesus does not in any way undermine his love for his fellow Jewish people, the people of Israel. On the contrary, Paul's experience of the love of Jesus magnifies his love and concern for his fellow Israelites, especially for those who do not yet know of or believe in Jesus. Paul clearly celebrates his identity as an Israelite (Rom. 11:1). Paul's identity as an Israelite remains: it is not lost, diluted or denied in becoming a follower of Jesus.

Paul is determined to show that God is faithful to his people Israel. Paul declares the eight blessings which belong to Israel (Rom. 9:4-5) and makes it clear that these blessings are all in the present tense; they have not been lost, or transferred to others. The terms 'Israel', 'people of Israel' or 'Israelite' are used by Paul as self–defining terms for all Jewish people. Paul uses the term 'Israelites' in Romans 9-11 deliberately rather than the term 'Jew' (which Paul uses in Romans 1-8) because the term 'Israelites' is religiously important and also it is an honorific title in the context of the history (and future) of God's purposes.

In Romans 9-11, Paul wrestles with the issue of Israel's calling and identity. In simple terms, chapter 9 deals with Israel's *selection* as God's people. This selection is as a result of God's sovereign choice. The choice is channelled through the promise of Isaac. It is made clear that this selection is to do with God's mercy and grace, not human merit or effort. Also in chapter 9, Paul deals with the promised calling of the Gentiles: Paul quotes from Hosea and Isaiah and shows that God's purpose equally includes Gentiles. This inclusion and affirmation of Gentiles clearly raises some related questions about God's faithfulness to and purposes for Israel.

In chapter 10, Paul deals with the current *stubbornness* of much of Israel which, although born out of a zeal for God, is not based on knowledge (Rom. 10:2). There is a clear understanding and passionate declaration that all Israelites who have not yet become followers of Jesus need to do so. In fact all people need to call on him and put their trust in him (Rom. 10:13) yet many Israelites refuse to respond. Again quoting from Isaiah, Paul calls Israel a 'disobedient and obstinate people' (Rom. 10:21).

In chapter 11, Paul deals with Israel's *salvation*. The current stubbornness of many Israelites and the apparent openness of many Gentiles to the saving message of Jesus, raises the question set out in Romans 11:1, namely has God now rejected Israel? This question hangs in the air – it marks a potential turning point in history; a paradigm shift may well occur. Sadly, much Christian theology answers the question with a resounding 'yes'. This has led to a tendency to view the church as the new Israel or the true spiritual Israel, which now replaces the old (ethnic) Israel within God's purposes. Sometimes this resounding 'yes' has also given room for antisemitic attitudes and actions to fester within the church.

However, Paul answers the question with a resounding 'no'!

For Paul, God has an ongoing plan for Israel. This plan begins with the faithful remnant within Israel (of which Paul sees himself as a member) and will continue through stubborn Israel being drawn back into the faithful remnant (Paul uses, in Rom. 11:11-24, the metaphor of natural branches being reconnected with the host [olive] tree and also connected alongside wild grafted-in branches). This will lead at some future point to all Israel being saved (Rom. 11:26), although how all of this will take place is not spelt out. However, Paul boldly concludes, in Romans 11, with a declaration of trust in and praise of God's sovereign power and wisdom (Rom. 11:33-36).

In conclusion, how God's purposes for Israel will be achieved and how Israel is viewed, is a contentious issue among many Jewish and Christian groups. There is much robust debate and there are many nuanced positions. However, I understand that for a correct reading of Paul's teaching on this subject, it is necessary to maintain a theology which emphasises continuity between the covenants and celebrates God's ongoing faithfulness to Israel. It is important that Israel is not redefined in such a way that allows the gospel to be severed from the hopes and promises of the patriarchs (Rom. 15:8). From my perspective, such a theology needs therefore to affirm the following five core points:

1. A clear distinction between the church and Israel needs to be maintained.

2. A clear affirmation of the role of Jewish believers in Jesus, both as members of Israel and as members of the church, needs to be proclaimed.

3. The unity of the church (Jew and Gentile united in Jesus) must be celebrated.

4. The ongoing faithfulness of God to Israel remains. The recreation of the Jewish state, for example, is a fulfilment of God's covenantal faithfulness.

5. The gospel must be shared lovingly and appropriately with Jewish people and non-Jewish people groups everywhere.

About the Contributors

Stephen Briggs

Stephen Briggs grew up in England, and at the age of nineteen he moved to Jerusalem where he was trained and discipled by the late Lance Lambert for four years. He has an extensive knowledge of the Middle East and a heart for sharing biblical truth.

In mid-2008 Stephen moved back to England to begin work with Hatikvah Film Trust, which promotes the advancement and understanding of the Christian faith and of Biblical prophecy through the production of documentary films and television programmes. Since then Stephen has also undertaken ministry engagements for other organisations and presented on Revelation TV.

Jacob Vince

Jacob has been Chief Executive of Christian Friends of Israel UK since 2010. He holds a master's degree in property valuation and law, and is by profession a chartered surveyor.

He worked in Israel on a kibbutz in the late 1970s and lived in Jerusalem in the early 1980s. He is a serving member of the General Synod of the Church of England and a Church Commissioner.

David Noakes

David read Law at Pembroke College, Oxford, and practised as a solicitor until called into full-time ministry in 1975. He has been an advisory board member of the European Coalition for Israel, which works in the European Parliament to support the nation of Israel. He was until recently a trustee and chairman of the board of Hatikvah Film Trust, a ministry which produces film documentaries designed to make known Biblical truths concerning the Jewish people and the land of Israel. He has also authored and co-authored three books: *Dynamic Prayer*; *Blessing the Church?*, a study of the development of the charismatic renewal movement; and *Israel, His People, His Land, His Story*, published by Love Never Fails.

Adam Raffell

Adam is from York and studied theology at St Andrews (M.Theol), as well as completing a postgraduate degree in Jewish-Christian relations through the Woolf Institute at Cambridge (M.St). He is the director of ministry development for Christians Care International, which is working to build a brighter future for Jewish people in need. Adam believes that Christians must recognise and affirm the validity of Jewish faith-practice without diluting Christian commitment to the good news about Jesus Christ. Working together, Christians and Jews can make the world a better place for all of humanity.

Rabbi Jonathan Allen

Jonathan is joint leader of Messianic Educational Trust (MET), an educational charity based in England and part of the Tikkun family of ministries, serving the Messianic Jewish community in Israel, Cyprus and the USA, as well as former republics of the Soviet Bloc. Jonathan is a member of the UK Towards Jerusalem Council II steering committee and was ordained as a Messianic rabbi in 2002. He is currently studying at Trinity College, Bristol for a PhD in Theology, focusing on the role of continuing Jewish identity in Jewish believers within the UK church.

Reverend Alex Jacob

Ordained as a minister of word and sacrament within the United Reformed Church in 1985, Alex was appointed as a director of The Church's Ministry among Jewish People (CMJ), before becoming CMJ's CEO in July 2011. He has a well-respected teaching and pastoral ministry and has been actively involved within the field of Jewish-Christian relations for many years. He holds an MA degree in Pastoral Theology from Cambridge Theological Federation/Anglia Ruskin University, and an MPhil research degree from Nottingham University. His research studies have been published by Glory to Glory publications in his book *The Case for Enlargement Theology*.

Bibliography

Some suggestions for further reading by chapter.

Chapter 1

Murray, John (1953) *The Covenant of Grace (A Biblico-theological Study)*, New Jersey: Presbyterian and Reformed Publishing Company.

Torrance, James B. (1970) 'Covenant or Contract: A Study of the Theological Background of Worship in Seventeenth-Century Scotland', *Scottish Journal of Theology*, 23(1), p51-76.

Quote: Watson, David (1978) *I Believe in the Church*, London: Hodder & Stoughton, p76.

Chapter 2

Glashouwer, Willem (2005) *Why Israel? New Beginnings*, Nijkerk, The Netherlands: Christians for Israel International.

Maltz, Steve (2003) *The Land of Many Names*, Milton Keynes, UK: Authentic Media.

Richards, Rob (2016) *Has God Finished with Israel?*, Preston, UK: Zaccmedia.

Vince, Jacob, *God's Land of Israel*, Eastbourne, UK: CFI Publications.

Vince, Jacob, *The Land Where Jesus Lived*, Eastbourne, UK: CFI Publications.

Vince, Jacob, *Was Jesus a Palestinian?*, Eastbourne, UK: CFI Publications.

Quote: Torrance, Thomas F. (1982) 'The Divine Vocation and Destiny of Israel in World History' *The Witness of the Jews to God*, ed. Torrance, David. W., Edinburgh: The Handsel Press, p85.

Chapter 3
Wright, Fred, ed. (2005) Section 5, 'The Restoration of All Things', *Israel, His People, His Land, His Story*, Eastbourne, UK: Thankful Books, p271.

Quote: Ryle, J.C. (1867) *Coming Events and Present Duties*, London: Prisbrary Publishing.

Chapter 4

Marquardt, Friedrich-Wilhelm, eds. Pangritz, A. and Chung, P.S., trans. McCord, D., Rumscheidt, H.M. and Chung, P.S. (2010) *Theological Audacities: Selected Essays*, Eugene, Oregon: Pickwick.

Torrance, David W., ed. (1982) *The Witness of the Jews to God*, Edinburgh: Handsel Press.

Quote: Marquardt, Friedrich-Wilhelm (1977) "'Enemies for Our Sake": The Jewish No and Christian Theology', *Theological Audacities: Selected Essays*, Eugene, Oregon: Pickwick, p19.

Chapter 5

Barth, Karl (1949) *Dogmatics in Outline* (especially chapter 11, 'The Saviour and Servant of God'), Norwich, UK: SCM Press.

Barth, Karl, eds. Bromiley, G.W. and Torrance, T.F. (1965-69) *Church Dogmatics*, Edinburgh: T & T Clark.

Moltmann, Jürgen (1990) *The Way of Jesus Christ: Christology in Messianic Dimensions*, Norwich, UK: SCM Press.

Quote: Barth, Karl (1949) *Dogmatics in Outline*, Norwich, UK: SCM Press, p74.

Chapter 6

Bockmuehl, Marcus (2000) *Jewish Law in Gentile Churches*, Edinburgh: T & T Clark.

Boyarin, Daniel (2012) *The Jewish Gospels*, New York, NY: The New Press.

Bruce, F.F. (1988) *The Book of the Acts (New International Commentary on the New Testament)*, Grand Rapids, MI: Eerdmans Publishing.

Shulam, Joseph and le Cornu, Hilary (2003) *The Jewish Roots of Acts*, Jerusalem: Academon.

Strellan, Rick (2008) *Luke the Priest*, Aldershot, UK: Ashgate.

Quote: Dobschiner, Johanna-Ruth (1982) 'Christ, the Fulfilment of the Jewish Faith', *The Witness of the Jews to God*, Torrance, David W. ed., Edinburgh: The Handsel Press, p127-128.

Chapter 7

Dunn, James (2011) *Jesus, Paul and the Gospels*, Grand Rapids, MI: Eerdmans Publishing.

Evans, David (2010) *Christians and Israel: The Heart of the Matter*, Jerusalem: Tahilla Press.

Jacob, Alex (2010) *The Case for Enlargement Theology*,

Saffron Walden, UK: Glory to Glory Publications.

Pawson, David (2009) *Israel in the New Testament*, London: Terra Nova Publications.

Santala, Risto (1995) *Paul: The Man and the Teacher*, Jerusalem: Keren Ahvah Meshihit Publications.

Skarsaune, Oskar and Hvalvik, Reidar, eds. (2007) *Jewish Believers in Jesus: The Early Centuries*, Peabody, MA: Hendrickson Publishers.

Quote: Moltman, Jürgen (1990) *The Way of Jesus Christ*, Norwich, UK: SCM Press, p36.

General further reading suggestions.

From a Contemporary 'Palestinianist' Perspective

Abu El-Assal, Riah (1999) *Caught in Between: The Story of an Arab Palestinian Christian Israeli*, London: SPCK.

Chacour, Elias (2013) *Blood Brothers: The Dramatic Story of a Palestinian Christian Working for Peace in Israel*, UK: Baker Books.

Chapman, Colin (2004) *Whose Holy City? Jerusalem and the Israeli-Palestinian Conflict*, Oxford: Lion Hudson.

Chapman, Colin (2004) *Whose Promised Land?*, Oxford: Lion Hudson.

Sizer, Stephen (2004) *Christian Zionism: Roadmap to Armageddon*, London: Inter-Varsity Press.

Sizer, Stephen (2007) *Zion's Christian Soldiers*, London: Inter-Varsity Press.

From a Historical Perspective
Crombie, Kelvin (2008) *For the Love of Zion: Christian Witness and the Restoration of Israel*, London: Terra Nova Publications.

Flavius, Josephus, ed. Smallwood, E. Mary, trans. Williamson, G. (1981) *The Jewish War*, London: Penguin Classics.

Segev, Tom (2001) *One Palestine Complete: Jews and Arabs Under the British Mandate*, London: Abacus.

Wilson, Marvin R. (1989) *Our Father Abraham: Jewish Roots of the Christian Faith*, Grand Rapids, MI: Eerdmans Publishing.

Ziff, William (2010) *The Rape of Palestine*, Eastford, CT: Martino Fine Books.

From a Contemporary Zionist Perspective

Kogan, Michael S. (2008) *Opening the Covenant: A Jewish Theology of Christianity*, Oxford: Oxford University Press.

Lambert, Lance (1980) *The Uniqueness of Israel*, Eastbourne, UK: Kingsway Publications.

Lambert, Lance (2007) *Jacob I Have Loved*, Lancaster, UK: Sovereign World.

Pawson, David (2008) *Defending Christian Zionism*, London: Terra Nova Publications.

Pawson, David (2014) *Israel in the New Testament*, Reading, UK: Anchor Recordings.

Sacks, Jonathan (2010) *Future Tense: A Vision for Jews and Judaism in the Global Culture*, London: Hodder & Stoughton.

Wilkinson, Paul (2007) *For Zion's Sake: Christian Zionism and the Role of John Nelson Darby*, Milton Keynes, UK: Paternoster.

Biblical Interpretation

Fee, Gordon D. and Douglas, Stuart (2014) *How to Read the Bible for All its Worth*, Grand Rapids, MI: Zondervan.

Hurtado, Larry (2005) *Lord Jesus Christ – Devotion to Jesus in Earliest Christianity*, Grand Rapids, MI: Eerdmans Publishing.

Soulen, R. Kendall (1996) *The God of Israel and Christian Theology*, Minneapolis, MN: Augsburg Fortress.